NEWGRANGE – TEMPL.

Newgrange
Temple to Life

Chris O'Callaghan

Mercier Press

MERCIER PRESS
Douglas Village, Cork
www.mercierpress.ie

Trade enquiries to COLUMBA MERCIER DISTRIBUTION,
55a Spruce Avenue, Stillorgan Industrial Park, Blackrock, Dublin

1 85635 428 8

10 9 8 7 6 5 4 3 2 1

DEDICATION
*To Barbara Barrett, artist and wifely, who sketched the illustrations
and
to the Boyne Valley People
who built a wondrous temple*

ACKNOWLEDGEMENTS
The internal photographs of Newgrange have been kindly made available by Dúchas. I also give a special thanks to Clare Tuffy, the manager of Brú na Bóinne.

Printed in Ireland by ColourBooks Ltd

Contents

1 – Where and When   7

2 – They call her a 'passage grave'   8

3 – The Newgrange Monument   12

4 – The Sun Window   19

5 – Lost and Found   29

6 – Refutable Logic in Action   34

7 – No Smoke No Fire   43

8 – No Bones No Burial   45

9 – The Celtic Connection   47

10 – The Boyne Valley People   50

11 – Life Expectancy   62

12 – The Four Seasons   64

13 – The Trigger   67

14 – The Plan   70

15 – You, the Leader   72

16 – The Farmer's View   77

17 – Building Her   79

18 – Fusion   83

19 – The Marriage   85

20 – Where did they go?   90

1

Where and When

Aerial view of Newgrange Monument

Perched on the forehead of a gentle ridge above the famous
River Boyne, 30 miles north of Dublin, capital city of the Irish
Republic, and hardly more than a cannon's shot from the still
smouldering 1690 battle between Catholic and Protestant,
stands one of the most enchanting and significant Neolithic
monuments of the ancient world – Newgrange.

Built by a highly developed and peaceful civilisation on
the western edge of the European continent over 5,000 years
ago, Newgrange predates the Great Pyramid at Giza by some
700 years.

2

They call her a 'passage grave'

Despite the accepted fact that Newgrange is one of the most advanced Neolithic constructions designed and built to manage the rays of the sun, many archaeologists persist with the 300 years old classification that Newgrange is merely a passage grave, or burial tomb; yet another of the many hundreds of so-called passage graves dotting the hills and plains of western Greater Europe.

A typical example of the portrayal of one of the wonders of the ancient world as a 'passage grave/burial tomb' is well illustrated by the entry on page 49 of the book, *Discovering Archaeology in England and Wales* by James Dyer, published by Shire Publications Ltd (1997), under the heading 'The Passage-Grave Builders':

Some time before 4000BC, a new type of great stone tomb, known as a passage grave, appeared in southern Brittany. Soon afterwards examples were appearing in Spain and Portugal and in Western Ireland. By 3000BC the idea had spread to north Wales.

Passage graves are circular mounds of earth or stone containing one or two round or polygonal burial chambers with corbelled roofs, entered from outside by long narrow passages. They are usually built on hilltops in commanding positions and are often grouped in cemeteries. The finest groups are in Ireland, where more than three hundred exist. They vary in size from … to the great tombs of the Boyne valley in County Meath, at Knowth, Dowth and New Grange. The last, now reconstructed, still stands at 12 metres high and between 80 and 85 metres in diameter, with the remains of a circle that once contained 38 great stones standing around it. Radiocarbon dates suggest that it was built about 3200BC.

The writer continues the common trend by not only describing and then discarding the Sun Window as 'a curious slot,' but also introduces, what I believe are, *five* inaccuracies in one sentence:

A curious slot in the roof of the entrance passage allows the sun for a *few* minutes at dawn on *a* midwinter's morning to enter the **burial** chamber and warm the **ashes** of the **dead**: surely a link with sun worship.

The sun's rays actually enter for seventeen minutes on each of twelve days, not for a 'few' on 'a' morning. In addition, the words 'burial', 'ashes' and 'dead' are unsubstantiated assumptions as no burial things, whether 'ashes' or 'the dead', have been found within the Newgrange monument.

Even overlooking the assumption of a burial chamber, an uninformed reader would not have the slightest idea that the information contains errors of fact and would expect that every thing was all present and correct.

While differing opinion is the oil of a functioning civilisation, in the so-called 'passage grave' context it appears that most authors and broadcasters have overlooked opportunities to even consider an alternative interpretation and choose rather to adopt the opinions of the fellow in front and follow their muddied and well trudged footsteps.

Despite the acknowledgement by respected academics that the Newgrange monument exhibits many remarkable and unique features, most books, leaflets and guides repeat the same safe and comfortable 'passage grave' story. I believe many academics and experts have gazed upon the huge mound with pre-programmed eyes – noting only the elements that fit the long-established interpretations, but ignoring the anomalies that suggest that the ancient edifice above the Boyne is much more than a common place of burial.

It is the contention of *Newgrange – Temple to Life* that the **traditional classification of the Newgrange monument as a common 'passage grave', but one with the Sun Window as an interesting add-on, is an oversight that should and can be rectified.** I propose further that the commonly coined 'passage grave/ burial tomb' description seriously misrepresents what the leaders, astronomers, architects, engineers, artists, builders, as well as the hundreds of workers, achieved on the Newgrange ridge over 5,000 years ago: a fusion of belief, astronomy, engineering and logistics that works as efficiently today as when declared open for business over 5,000 years ago.

A wondrous monument was created by an advanced civilisation, as yet unrecognised, that had taken root on the western edge of the European continent, at a similar time to when the first Mesopotamian city states were forming between the Tigris and the Euphrates.

You are invited therefore, to peruse the following pages which explore the why and the how the great monument was constructed. At first there is a brief description of what had been built at Newgrange long ago. This is followed by a touch of history to show how the inaccurate moniker, 'passage grave', came to blight Newgrange. Finally, *Newgrange – Temple to Life* proposes a fresh and thought-provoking insight and explanation into the life or death drama that drove the Boyne Valley People to build the world's most advanced monument of its time.

3

The Newgrange Monument

Montage of Newgrange scenes

On arrival at the site of the ancient monument, you will be faced by a massive 200,000 ton, grass-topped and drum-shaped, hand-built mound that occupies a full acre (half hectare), and is over 40 feet (12 metres) high. The construction is in prime condition following the careful and professional restoration that took advantage of the combination of the original sturdy construction, limited storm damage and powerful superstition that kept would-be vandals at bay.

The great mound was completely necklaced by 96 massively heavy kerbstones of which ...

... some kerbstones, K52 ...

... and K67, were artistically carved.

The famous entrance stone

A ninety-seventh kerbstone is the famous entrance stone. However before your gaze starts to settle on the details of the imposing monument, you will notice that the mound is sur-

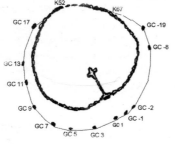

rounded by a guard of massive boulders – the much photographed Standing Stones.

The twelve Standing Stones form an incomplete circle that is not equidistant from the mound. This circle impinges on the northern curve, between two of the most decorated kerbstones, K52 and K67. Excavations under the direction of David Sweetman showed that the Standing Stones were placed in position after the monument had been completed. Their positioning has suggested the possibility of astro-archaeological events, whereby the juxtaposition of monument and the Standing Stones could have formed a seasonal calendar that had agricultural as well as ceremonial significance. Identified as local post-glacial erratics, the 2 to 2.5 metres tall Standing Stones were undecorated.

Regarding the breaks in the circle, although the gaps suggest that up to 38 stones once completed the circle, diligent searching has revealed no disused stone sockets. Possibly the twelve stones achieved all the ancients needed for their seasonal calculations.

The dramatic, south facing, 3 metre (10 ft) tall reflective fascia wall is formed by bright white quartz rocks, interspersed with melon-size water-rolled boulders. However, before entering the magic mound and falling under her spell, a hint of caution may be in order. Although an advanced people, some writers have credited the ancient builders with astrological achievements that common sense should tell us were far beyond their impressive development.

Quartz fascia

Entrance

The enticing entrance to the passage and end-chamber is located in the middle of the quartz fascia. The entrance, and the Sun Window built immediately above, were perfectly aligned by the ancient Irish builders to receive the dawn rays of the mid-winter December sun, the winter solstice in the northern hemisphere. Remarkable features within the New-grange mound include the cleverly roofed, 19 metre (60 foot) long, and one metre wide, stone-lined passage.

Passage

End-chamber

The passage leads directly to the spacious 30 square metre end-chamber – a room almost 300 square feet in area.

Three alcoves flank this end-chamber – each holding large, basin-shaped stones within enigmatically etched walls.

Alcove and stone basin

Corbelled roof of the end-chamber

The end-chamber is also characterised by a brilliantly corbelled roof that rises some six metres (20 feet) above the grit-covered floor. This is the oldest corbelled roof discovered, so far, in the Old World, superseding those found in Egypt

An often-overlooked accolade to the builders is that the passage and end-chamber were so well constructed that for over 5,000 years they have remained quite dry. Stepped passage roof-stones and painstakingly chipped gullies, successfully drained percolating rainwater from the notoriously damp Atlantic weather. The seams and joins were further waterproofed with a putty of ash and sea sand which is remarkably similar to a modern mix of a burnt lime cement and river sand.

4

The Sun Window

Sun Window

However, it is the design, installation and workings of the unique Sun Window, named the 'roof-box' by the late Professor Michael O'Kelly, that really lifts the Newgrange monument into a class of her own; an innovation that should cause a visitor to ponder long and deep when offered the standard 'passage grave' description.

It is, in fact, the *modus operandi* of the Sun Window that provides the first real clue to why the Boyne Valley People planned to build a monument many planes above a common passage grave. For reasons that are explained later, the Boyne Valley People required the rays of the sun to penetrate to the end-chamber, the nethermost and most private part of the monument. However, only the dawn rays from the northern hemisphere winter solstice sun, for six days either side of 21 December were invited to enter the Sun Window.

Although the entrance to the passage and end-chamber was discovered in 1699, either having been sealed by purposeful collapse, or weather-induced erosion of part of the encircling wall and covering mound some 4,000 years earlier, the Sun Window was not recognised and released from incarceration until the late 1960s. A remarkable delay when there were at least two widely known clues that suggested a direct relation between winter and the sun's rays reaching down the passage.

One hint was a local rumour that claimed that at some time during the year, the sun's rays touched the pillars standing at the threshold of the end-chamber. The other pointer emanated from the respected Sir Norman Lockyer. In 1909, he suggested that the monument was oriented towards the Winter Solstice. Neither clue was tested!

Ironically the leading edge of the lintel of the Sun Window had been peaking from the rubble, weeds and small bushes for a very long time without being investigated, until the major 1962–75 renovation. This oversight proved to be a blessing in disguise as it preserved the Sun Window to be uncovered and semi-restored by a professional team, rather than a greedy souvenir hunter, or worse.

Leading edge of the lintel of the Sun Window

In fact, it was only during the 1969 Winter Solstice, on 21 December from 08h.58 until 09h.15, 270 years after the entrance had been re-opened, that the full interaction of the dawn rays of the Winter Solstice sun on the end-chamber was timed and recorded by modern witnesses (pp. 123–124 in *Newgrange* by Michael J. O'Kelly, Thames and Hudson 1982).

In 20:20 hindsight, it was an excellent opportunity to recognise what the ancients had actually constructed upon their Newgrange ridge and to release the mighty monument from the dark and undeserved shrouds of the mournful Cult of the Dead.

When the Sun Window was first cleared of rubble during the 1962–75 restoration, an unusual find, a block of quartz, was discovered within the aperture. Scratch marks on the surfaces of the underlying slabs of rock that formed the floor of the Sun Window (and the roof of the entrance and passage below), showed that originally the block was one of a twin. At the time, Professor O'Kelly decided that the quartz block was of little significance and, together with the missing partner, had been merely used to close off the Sun Window when not in use.

However, a number of independent researchers have subsequently argued convincingly that the quartz blocks would have provided a far more dramatic input than O'Kelly ever imagined. It is well known that quartz, or silicone dioxide, is a mineral that possesses a number of exciting properties. Every nano-second, millions of timepieces and computers are utilising quartz's unique properties. Not only can quartz split light into the full rainbow of colours, it can also store and release energy that is directional and pulsating. In other words, when the Winter Solstice sun passed through the quartz blocks that had been placed tightly in the Sun Window, the end-chamber could have been filled with an energised rainbow that was releasing energy into the surrounding farm-land.

In the Newgrange context, this most interesting possibility cannot be tested as the recently discovered surviving quartz block, safe for 5,000 years, has apparently been mislaid in less than forty. But if refraction, or polarisation, did in fact occur, the end-chamber could have been filled with an event that would amaze even the most blasé twenty-first century visitor and lead to all manner of interesting questions being aimed at academia.

Would it be too much to hope that one day a benefactor will provide funds for two replacement quartz blocks to be crafted and the energising phenomenon professionally tested?

It can also be wondered whether the quartz rocks, randomly placed during the restoration to form the fascia of the mound, had not originally been placed 'directionally' so as to 'pass-on' the energy absorbed from the sun-of-the-day throughout the year.

In ancient times quartz had been described as 'The Ice of the Gods' and 'Sun Stones', both suggesting that some of the properties of the mineral were well known to the builders of Newgrange. An intriguing possibility!

Whether some consider that quartz-promoted energisation is a beam too far, nevertheless you might wonder why a so-called common 'passage grave' would be fitted with an attachment designed to select the sun's rays from only twelve of 365 days and beam the rays directly onto a selected target, year after year. The Sun Window is so well built that it can still perform this action more than 5,000 years later and at a time of the year when the sun's rays are coolest and facing a good chance of being drowned by rain.

Regarding the choice of the Winter Solstice Sun, you may also have wondered why the bolder, brighter and brash mid-summer sun had not been invited to swamp the end-chamber. Surely, you may have thought, the summer sun would offer a better chance of a decent dawn and longer, more pleasant days for ceremonies.

However, for reasons that will be given later, it would seem that the Boyne Valley People had been compelled to stage the unique dawn ceremony at a time of the year when their world was at its least fertile – when the food chain was hanging by the weakest links. I can only conclude that the motivating factor was very powerful, or very frightening, to have persuaded, or forced, the ancients to fight their way out of bed during the bleakest time of the year, to harness the rays of the comparatively soft winter sun.

But before we discover what spurred the Boyne Valley People to build the massive mound, let us work out how the Sun Window was planned and placed to guarantee the solar invasion of Newgrange's 24 metre (80 feet), passage and end-chamber, at dawn for twelve mornings every December.

As modern researchers discover more and more about the construction of the monument, especially in relation to other geographical features, it seems very unlikely that the designer of the monument left the spot, where the first rays of the Winter Solstice Sun would touch the Newgrange ridge, to random chance. In other words, the point on the Newgrange ridge where the dawn sun first touched the earth, became the focal point of the monument, a point that would later be occupied by the stone basin that is still nestling in the middle alcove of the end-chamber. Once the focal point on the ridge had been fixed, the orientation of the passage, that would ultimately control the dawn rays of the northern Winter Solstice Sun, could then be determined.

In order to have any chance of achieving this prerequisite, the ancients would require advanced knowledge of the movements of the sun as well as an accurate year-on-year calendar. The fact that the Sun Window is still operational, over 5,000 years after installation, provides acceptable proof that the Boyne Valley People were well versed in at least the prime celestial movements.

As mentioned earlier, while the precise spot on the Newgrange ridge, where the dawn rays of the Winter Solstice Sun should fall, had been marked, so too would the winter sun's rising point on the far south-eastern horizon need to be noted. In effect, both the start and end points of the first rays of the Solstice Sun had to be precisely plotted.

By using a simple 'V' cut into a sighting-stick, a straight line would have been plotted and scratched on the ground of the Newgrange hill, towards the chosen focal point. In effect, this line would provide the vital direction and positioning of the passage stones, from entrance to the end-chamber.

However, if ascertaining when the shortest day/longest night would occur, and then plotting the line between the point of the rise of the dawn sun and the desired focal point were tricky, further complications were added to the designers' list. For a reason that will be revealed later, the elders of the Boyne Valley People would stipulate that the meeting of the first rays of the Winter Solstice sun and the focal point, which was where the stone basin in the middle alcove would be later positioned, had to take place out of sight of the general populace. It was a demand that the designers and engineers could not ignore, despite including two diametrically opposing elements. Because the early morning sun would, obviously, be low on the dawn horizon, the beams would be blocked by any wall that might be built to prevent the gathered clans from observing the rays actually touching the focal point, the stone basin in the middle alcove.

In effect, the design team had to find a way of bending the sunlight so that the sun's rays would neither be blocked when the clans gathered for the various ceremonies, nor when the alcoves, the end-chamber, the passage and the Sun Window had all been built.

This was an challenging problem to solve a thousand or so years before mirrors arrived in Neolithic Ireland. But solve the problem they did and you can see their solution above the entrance to the passage and end-chamber at Newgrange.

The Sun Window above the entrance

Sun Window above the entrance

The Sun Window was a brilliant innovation, conceived, designed and built in Ireland – and not imported or adapted from civilisations to the east. In order to ensure that there were no obstructions to the flow of the dawn rays from the horizon to the middle alcove-to-be, the designers used the slope of the hill to move the people two metres out of the way. At a particular point down the forehead of the hill, some 22 metres from where the middle stone basin would one day sit, the designers marked where the 'eye' of the planned Sun Window picked up the line-of-sight between the horizon and the previously chosen focal point. Where the line-of-sight passed through the 'eye' provided the position and direction, both horizontally and vertically, where the Sun Window would be constructed.

In effect, the Sun Window could now be precisely positioned, in both direction and declination, so that only selected dawn rays of the winter sun could enter the dedicated opening to gently touch the base of the middle alcove. Once this position of the Sun Window had been checked and re-checked for accuracy, lines for the two ranks of stones that would form the passage to the end-chamber could be marked and sockets cut in the ground. At the same time, the precise dimensions of the end-chamber and the three flanking alcoves could also be marked and construction on the great monument commence.

I suggest, therefore, that the Sun Window was not just the interesting attachment, or quaint innovation, noted in passing by many historians and archaeologists, mesmerised by the standing stones, the carved kerbstones and orthostats lining the passage. Nor was this aperture merely an interesting slot, as some would have it. *I argue that the Sun Window provides the key for the reason for building the Newgrange monument.* Before the Sun Window had been designed and her position determined, nothing else could have been placed in position.

When visiting the monument, visitors will be advised that the floor of the passage follows the natural inclination of the hill and rises by two metres, from the entrance to the end-chamber. This rise was to ensure that an assembled crowd would not obstruct the passage of the dawn sun and to allow the sun's rays to perform a required task in privacy and without undue interruption.

In the context of privacy, it is noted that the walls of the passage to the end-chamber do not follow an expected straight line. As you enter the passage you will find yourself first turning to the right and then to the left. In effect, the curves, plus

Diagram of the side view of the stones and line of the sun's beam during the Winter Solstice

Interior of the sun window during the Winter Solstice

the two metre rise in the passage floor, from entrance to end-chamber, block any view of the end-chamber from the entrance, preserving the privacy of whatever occurred within the end-chamber during the Winter Solstice. This brilliant design solution guarantees the solar invasion of the 24-metre long (80 feet) passage and end-chamber at dawn, for six days on either side of the 21 December Winter Solstice. Each early morning penetration lasts for a maximum of seventeen minutes – softly bathing the end-chamber and the stone offering-basins within the three alcoves with an ethereal light.

Yet, despite the imaginative and innovative Sun Window, Newgrange is still referred to as a passage grave – a classification that has become generic with usage and is apparently set in stone!

However, is the reluctance to replace a tired, 300-year-old classification not risking missing an exciting and more likely interpretation? An explanation that fits the front-of-face evidence accurately and is straightforward and uncomplicated and more convincing than the out-of-date guess that the monument is only a passage grave, though one with an interesting attachment!

5

Lost and Found

The first official classification of Newgrange as a burial tomb can be traced to 1699, the year when Newgrange landowner, Charles Campbell, decided to repair a local road. Believing there was a large quantity of suitable stones beneath a particularly large mound on his land, Campbell instructed a gang of labourers to extract what they could. Whether by luck or the timely intervention of resident guardian spirits, before a destruction similar to that at nearby Dowth megalithic monument, two strokes of good fortune saved the Newgrange monument for posterity.

As the pickaxes and crowbars commenced to harry and hack at the bush and tree infested mound, a large boulder was uncovered on which a mysterious pattern of squirls had been painstakingly chipped and carved. It was a stone so boldly unusual that even the most unlettered labourer could discern a 'stop' sign.

Entrance stone

Five thousand years after being carefully levered into place, and subsequently mislaid for some 4,000 years, the famous entrance stone at Newgrange had been uncovered. As the gang gathered to gaze upon the strange manifestation and the youngest and fleetest was dispatched to fetch Mr Campbell to rule on the amazing discovery, a second stroke of good fortune occurred. A respected Welsh scholar and antiquarian,

Edward Lhwyd, happened to be in the Co. Meath neighbourhood. Receiving news of 'the find' he was quickly on hand to support the landowner's instincts to preserve the mound and whatever it might contain. The following entry appears on

Edward Lhwyd

page 30 in *New Grange* by Seán P. Ó Ríordáin and Glyn Daniel (Thames & Hudson 1964) regarding the professional credentials of Mr Lhwyd:

> It has been said that New Grange is the most well known of the pre-historic sites in the Bend of the Boyne, and it was naturally New Grange which attracted the earliest travellers who have left accounts of their antiquarian travels in Ireland. The first of these was the Welsh antiquary Edward Lhwyd (1660–1708), a man who was described by Sir John Rhys as 'in many respects the greatest Celtic philologist the world has ever seen', but who was also, with his contemporary John Aubrey, in many ways the founder of modern field archaeology.
>
> Lhwyd was a polymath in the true seventeenth-century use of that term; he travelled widely in Celtic countries observing the manners and customs of the people, their language, their antiquities, and the natural world in which they lived.

Lhwyd must, indeed, have been well respected. Sir Isaac Newton financed the publication of one of his books. He was also granted an honorary masters degree from Oxford University and later elected to be an Esquire Beadle of Divinity. In short, Mr Lhwyd was an experienced and interested observer, well equipped to record anything of note that he encountered on his travels . He was perfectly suited for his enviable role as the first academically accomplished person to enter the Newgrange passage and end-chamber in something like 4,000 years. In fact, as the Ashmolean paid him nothing for his duties, Mr Lhwyd's income was solely dependent on his reputation as an accurate researcher and philologist.

On the other hand, it can be shown that Mr Lhwyd's interpretations, as opposed to his observations, were heavily influenced by the attitudes and beliefs of his time. For example, in the first letter after his Newgrange visit, to a Dr Tancred Robinson, on 15 December 1699, Lhwyd's description of entering the monument runs as follows:

> At the first entering, we were forced to creep; but still as we went on, the pillars on each side of us were higher and higher; and coming into the cave we found it about 20 foot high.*
>
> In this cave, on each hand of us was a cell or apartment, and another went straight forward opposite to the entry. In those on each hand was a very broad shallow bason (sic) of stone, situated at the edge. The bason in the right hand apartment stood in another; that on the left was single, and in the apartment straight forward there was none at all.

Up until this point Mr Lhwyd's notes are without colour. His observation that there was no stone basin in the middle alcove

*cave: undermound or underground chambers were described by academics as caves.

being later attributed to the possibility that he did not notice that the floor-stone within the alcove was the apparently missing stone basin. Unfortunately, in the next part of the letter Mr Lhwyd was unable to resist adding a touch of modern style spin:

> We observed that water dropt into the right hand bason, tho' it had rained but little in many days; and suspected that the lower bason was intended to preserve the superfluous liquor of the upper (whether this water was sacred, or whether it was for Blood in Sacrifice) that none might come to the ground.

Having introduced the charged thought of Blood Sacrifice – and the brackets are part of the quote – then later describing the designs carved into the stones within the passage and end-chamber as 'barbarous', the Welsh antiquarian had done the lasting damage. However, he did go on to mention a gold coin of the Emperor Valentinian that had been found outside the mound and was at least able to attribute the monument correctly:

> So, the coin proving it ancienter than any Invasion of the Ostmans or Danes, and the carving and rude sculpture, barbarous; It should follow, that it was some place of sacrifice or burial of the ancient Irish.

Amazingly enough, the coin on the outside, and the 'barbarous' etchings on the inside, did not deflect Mr Lhwyd from reaching a remarkable bipolar observation. One, that the ancient Irish were the ones involved with Newgrange, being highly perceptive and correct; the second, in which he introduced 'sacrifice' and the dreaded 'burial' word, thus dooming Newgrange to be slotted as a passage grave for 300 years. This is a view without substantiation then, but one that is still common in this age despite many conclusions from earlier times being successfully questioned and changed.

It would seem that Mr Lhwyd's Irish-only insight, when coupled with the word 'burial', so confused academics, that they ignored the correct Irish-built first half, but knelt blindly before Lhwyd's second supposition, that Newgrange was a burial site and therefore a passage grave. The truth of Irish construction was out the window and forgotten, but the blarney of a burial site was in. A naïve one-size-fits-all envelope, but one that, despite dramatically advanced equipment, research facilities, instant communications and a much vaster range of information, remains unchanged, even into the twenty-first century.

6

Refutable Logic in Action

Examination of eighteenth and nineteenth century books reveal that the suggestion that the Irish could have built Newgrange had been rejected as fanciful. This attitude is attributable to the Rule Britannia syndrome living within the British empire then encircling on the maps of the world. Many of the reputedly learned and wise of these two centuries held that the Irish would have been quite incapable of conceiving, let alone designing and building, the massive and complex structure on the Newgrange hill. Such an achievement could only have been the work of the Egyptians, the Romans, ancient Indians, and Norsemen. What about the Greeks, the Basques or the Bulgars? Anyone, dear Henry, but not the Irish!

Ironically, the same academics, well-read and reputedly learned and wise fellows, ensconced in their safe ivory towers, overlooked the fact that for a thousand years, during and following the Dark Ages, when England was under the mud, Irish monasteries, missionaries and teachers kept the candles of European learning and creativity flickering bravely in the face of vandal assault. In addition, from the opening of Newgrange in 1699, until the end of the first quarter of the twentieth century, the rule of the British Raj meant that in most matters academic, what the English-speaking establishment believed was what the English-speaking world believed. During that time, much of Ireland lay under colonial rule.

While the gaining of freedom in the 1920s provided the opportunity for Ireland to reclaim at least the building of Newgrange, sadly the passage grave/burial tomb label stuck. Except in a few enlightened corners, the tomb sobriquet remains as sticky as ever.

The continuation of the crude application of the passage grave/burial tomb classification to blanket the thousands of pre-Christian stone markers and monuments that dot Iberia, Ireland, France and the United Kingdom can be traced to the earliest days of the 'ologies'. The reasoning of the time and one that has been carried relentlessly through to today, is quite simple – when a pile of large stones had been collected and arranged more or less neatly by people from ancient history, what had been built must be broadly classified into one of only three categories – (1) military and defence, (2) church and domestic, (3) passage grave or burial tomb.

The Welsh visitor to Newgrange, Edward Lhwyd, and later

academics, would see the covering mound, note the Standing Stones and followed the simple formula. Ancient people had undoubtedly constructed the monument. Large stones had certainly been arranged as a passage, terminating in a cruciform configuration. The shape was familiar and by simple elimination could be quickly sorted into one of the three categories: *viz.* military and defence; church and domestic; passage grave or burial tomb.

The mound on the Newgrange hill showed no defensive characteristics, so it was obviously not a fort. Neither could the patently pre-St Patrick, windowless and chimney-less mound allow classification as church or domestic habitation. Therefore, to the scholars of the eighteenth century and apparently nearly all those who have followed, the monument resembled nothing other than a classic passage grave or burial tomb. This categorisation is so broad that it would be just as sensible to classify all urban vehicles as taxis, or all fields enclosed by stadia as soccer pitches.

Interestingly, four of Mr Lhwyd's letters referring to Newgrange still exist. All reported quantities of animal bones within the passage and end-chamber, but despite detailed descriptions, in not one of his letters did Mr Lhwyd suggest the presence of human bones. Though many years later, fragments of human bones, mixed with the grit and sand, were discovered on the floor of the passage and end-chamber, at the time of his entry, although Lhwyd incorrectly assumed burial, he could offer neither bone nor body nor the flimsiest evidence.

Apart from a few stag horns and animal bones, Lhwyd did not record anything suggesting burial lying within the stone basins, on the floor of the passage or the end-chamber. Nothing burial-like stuffed between the sentinel orthostats lining the interior of the mound – no clay pots, empty or otherwise. To Mr Lhwyd's practised eye, even the stone basins were clear of burial goods.

There was no sign then, or later, that Newgrange had been used as a catacomb, a mortuary, necropolis, royal or otherwise, or a crematorium. Despite the assumptions, there is not the faintest evidence that Newgrange had ever been used as any sort of dedicated repository for bodies, bones, burial artefacts or ash. Nor have the interpretations* been able to show that any of the patterns carved into the stones signify death or burial in any way. Despite the mantra of modern academia, the application of 'grave or tomb' to Newgrange is unsupportable.

Indeed, mention of finding burial goods has only ever been based on assumptions. No traces of burial goods have ever been found. In addition, the stone basins have never shown any signs of the slightest bloodstains – surely an expected indicator after a 1,000 years of claimed slaughter and sacrifice. In contrast, one of the characteristics of Newgrange was the complete absence of pottery, whole or broken, that could have stored human remains. It would seem that the grim reaper never made the Newgrange guest list.

In the otherwise definitive and excellent book, *Newgrange* by Michael J. O'Kelly (Thames and Hudson 1998), a serious assumption appears in chapter two, p. 25:

> When the tomb was entered in 1699 it is probable that the
> deposits of cremated bone and the grave-goods, which had

---

* *See* Irish Symbols of 3500BC *by N. L. Thomas, Mercier Press 1988*

been originally placed in the basins, were *brushed aside or ignored in the quest for the more prestigious type of find* with which 'caves' were associated in the popular imagination.

I suggest that the assumption of the possibility of bone, cremated or otherwise, or so-called grave goods, within the stone basins, is a will-o'-the-wisp conjecture, and that the sentence has no place in an otherwise brilliant book in the name of a talented man who led a skilful restoration. The unsubstantiated comment illustrates that even in modern times, respected archaeologists experience difficulty bringing themselves to eschew the habits of traditional categorisation. Unsurprising then the academics of the 1800s and 1900s, unaided by information that is widely available today, but heavily influenced by precedent and the teachings of their elders and 'betters,' did not question Mr Lhwyd's passage grave appellation.

After all, to the antiquarians of the time, Newgrange had been built within a broad geographical area populated by similar ancient people, following broadly similar customs – amongst which was the construction of mounds and barrows of which some, though not by any means all, gave rest to human bones and ash.

However, at no time have reports, or even later excavations, shown that there were any signs of the purposeful storage of human bones and ash within the Newgrange monument.

The occurrence of the odd fragments of human bones will be explained later.

Curiously, a plan of the interior of Newgrange, drawn for Mr Lhwyd in 1700CE, shows a coned stone, described as follows: 'A stone wrought in the form of a Cone, half a yard long

and about 20 inches in the Girth, having a small
hole in the big end. This ... within the right hand
Cistern under the basin above mentioned.' While
the whereabouts of this stone is now as unknown
as the missing block of quartz, we could wonder
how the ancients were able to drill a hole into a
cone of stone. Notwithstanding, a conical stone with a neat
hole sounds remarkably like a pendulum – an interesting line
of thought developed by Hugh Kearns.*

Despite a hiatus in the use of the monument for thousands of years until the re-opening in 1699, and ignoring the
unsubstantiated claim that 'deposits ... were brushed aside',
because Mr Lhwyd did not report otherwise, we must accept
that the three stone basins in the alcoves did *not* contain
burial material when he first examined them. After all, Mr
Lhwyd has never been accused of being a grave robber, a
bounty hunter or seeking personal aggrandisement – his track
record was of a dedicated academic.

Regarding the insertion of creative observations, the archa-
eologically definitive book *Newgrange* does query a somewhat
lurid report from a Sir Thomas Molyneux, published in 1726,
some years after his visit to Newgrange. Described as Professor
of Physick in the University of Dublin, Sir Thomas apparently
succumbed to the temptation to give his article a more dramatic appeal by writing the following version of Lhwyd's visit:

> when the cave was first opened, the bones of two dead bodies
> entire, not burnt, were found upon the floor, in likelyhood
> the reliques of a husband and his wife, whose conjugal affec-
> tions had joyn'd them in their grave, as in their bed.

* See pp. 69–73 of The Mysterious Chequered Lights of Newgrange by Hugh
Kearns, Elo Publications 1993

This quote could have found an excellent bed-fellow in the form of a photograph on the front page of a tabloid and accompanied by a suitably provocative banner headline.

While some animal horns and bones, though not human bones, were noted lying on the floor of the Newgrange passage when Edward Lhwyd first entered in 1699, one would expect the sober antiquarian to notice and record a pair of skeletons locked in lover's embrace. Especially as the layout of the passage and end-chamber would have forced Mr Lhwyd to either crawl, or creep over, the romantically inclined bones. (Indeed, how was Sir Thomas able to decide that the phantom skeletons were married?) Nevertheless, had there been a skeleton or two, surely, Mr Lhwyd would have noted the spectacle as it is unlikely that skeletonised lovers would often be encountered in the normal course of the average academic's travels. But the point is that Molyneux's wild assumption is another unsubstantiated association of the Newgrange monument with doom, tomb and death.

Regarding the very few and mostly fragmented human bones found within the monument, the 1962–75 researchers record that their minute and careful examination suggests that in total, parts of only five persons were counted – two unburned and three cremated. T. P. Fraher of the Department of Anatomy at the University College Cork (*Newgrange*, Appendix B, page 197) notes the following under the heading, 'Unburnt Material':

> The samples containing unburnt human material also included large numbers of animal bones as well as about 750 unidentifiable fragments. Apart from some complete hand and foot bones, all human specimens consisted of small fragments.

Laboratory tests that followed the excavation and restoration of the mound did not seem to have conclusively dated the human bones. Certainly, no link was suggested, let alone established, between the human bones and the date when Newgrange was in use.

That there were a few human bones within the monument is not questioned. But as an overwhelming proportion of the bones discovered were unidentified fragments or animal bones, to classify the few human fragments as human burial material is surely an unsafe assumption. As the researchers of the eighteenth and nineteenth centuries did not have access to anything like the equipment of today, they had no means of ascertaining from where, or when, the scattered bones had arrived, or even how they arrived inside the monument. Therefore, reaching an incorrect conclusion as to the original use of the monument would be unsurprising.

There is, however, a straightforward explanation as to how a few well-fragmented human bones would have arrived within the mound. After many hundreds of years in use, and for whatever the reason, the Boyne Valley People abandoned the great monument. It is quite possible that at this time, and before the partially collapsed mound completely covered the entry points, wild animals could have entered the unguarded monument. To the animals, oblivious of custom and taboo, the empty passage and end-chamber would have offered an enticing hidey-hole and perfect lair. Agile carnivores would have encountered little difficulty sliding their sinuous bodies between the debris of the collapsing curtain wall and mound to find a safe refuge, carrying body parts, a few human, mostly animal, that the beasts had scavenged, an easy and natural likelihood. Their powerful jaws chomped and fragmented the bones to the state in which they were discovered 4,000 years later.

But so far as the passage grave classification is concerned, there is no hint that the pieces of fragmented bone, discovered mixed with the sand and grit on the floor of the monument, can be even remotely linked to sacrifice or burial activities.

No advanced dating device or technique has indicated that any of the bones and ash found within the mound have been dated to between 3200BCE and 2200BCE, when Newgrange was in use.

Accepted evidence has shown that by the time the next 'locals' arrived to settle Newgrange, the so-called Beaker People, the entrance to the monument had disappeared under a slide of debris from the covering mound. Hence the contents of the monument were not affected by subsequent settlers, whether Beaker, Celt, Norse, Norman or English, until 1699CE, when Mr Lhwyd entered the scene. It would be fair, therefore, to state that a passage grave without the requisite burial material is either suffering from a major oversight, or *never was a passage grave*.

Please note that, in deference to non-Christian readers, BCE, Before Common Era and CE, Common Era, are used instead of BC and AD.

7

No Smoke No Fire

View from inside middle alcove towards the passage

Before leaving the interior of the magic mound, it should be mentioned that when first opened, neither the walls nor the ceiling of the passage, the end-chamber or its flanking alcoves, exhibited any signs of burnt sacrifices within the monument. Apart from expected debris later left by visitor's candles, there was no evidence of fire, half-burnt twigs, an altar or fireplace – nothing to suggest cremations. With the lack of ventilation, to attempt a decent fire within the confines would likely lead to disappointment or asphyxiation.

When the mound was re-opened in 1699, the stone basins showed no signs of anything having been burnt within their hollows. Had there been cremations, these would have taken place outside the monument. As the Boyne Valley People occupied the Newgrange area for a considerable period, at least upwards of a thousand years, a significant number of bodies would have required some sort of disposal.

In other words, if the Newgrange monument had been used in any way for the cremation, or the storage of human bones or ash, during the millennium that passed before the Boyne Valley People moved away, there should be considerable evidence of burials and cremations within the passage and the end-chamber.

There are no signs now, nor was there ever, any such evidence.

The reasonable conclusion would surely be that while the Boyne Valley People obviously found an efficient means of disposing of their dead, cremation and or internment of bodies and bones within the Newgrange monument was not one of them.

Therefore, on what grounds can the monument be referred to as a passage grave!

8

No Bones No Burial

To clear the air and the memory of any remaining doubts of classifying the Newgrange monument as a passage grave, let us approach the question from the side of the expert establishment. Let us discover how well the monument, in use for almost a thousand years, would have performed as the passage tomb that academia avers it to be.

Question: What would you expect to find within a passage grave/tomb?

	Newgrange Score
1. Human skeletons, mummies, skulls, major bones. i.e., a catacomb-like place of storage.	None
2. Receptacles, usually of pottery, containing bones and ash.	None
3. Built-in repositories for bones, bone ash, burial goods.	Poor*
4. Burial goods.	None
5. Art and decorations suggesting death, sacrifice or burial.	None
6. Evidence of cremations within the passage and end-chamber.	None
7. Evidence of the theft of burial goods since 2200BCE.	None**

---

* *The stone basins within the three alcoves are closer to shallow shelves designed to provide temporary places for non-sacrificial ceremonial offerings.*
** *The interior was sealed by partial collapse of the covering mound from about 2200BCE, until the re-opening in 1699CE, at which time Edward Lhwyd made a careful note of the reported and personally observed contents. It is unlikely that superstitious road-workers would have removed human bones or ash without some hint reaching the antiquarian.*

8. Evidence of an alternate use of the monument.   Yes***

The foregoing check raises the obvious question regarding the building of the monument at Newgrange. For what purpose did the Boyne Valley People expend so much energy and time to raise her?

But before exploring the mass of evidence – material and circumstantial – to find the answer, there is a popular misconception that should be quickly put to rest – the so-called *Celtic* connection with the Newgrange monument.

*** *Described in the closing pages.*

9

The Celtic Connection

The common assumption, so loved by historians and poets, romancers and re-incarnators of ancient rites, is that there is some sort of link between the origin of the Newgrange monument and the religious arm of the Celts, the cowelled and seemingly threatening Druids. This connection has been given substance by allocating a Celtic appellation, 'Brú na Bóinne', the Mansion by the Boyne, to the modern Interpretative Centre near Donore. This myth has been

The druid

Brú na Bóinne

further coloured with bold claims by modern Druids that the interior of the monument was a place of ancient Celtic worship. Unfortunately for these claims, the partial collapse of the covering mound and the sealing of the entrance took place a thousand years before the first Celtic settlers crossed to Ireland, hence entry would not have been possible.

However, it is perfectly likely that the highly intelligent and knowledgeable Druids would have incorporated the signs

Newgrange mound before the 1962–75 restoration

and symbols of the Boyne Valley People, and their off-shoots encountered in Europe, into their customs.

There are also the myths in which one of the groups of early settlers, the Tuatha de Dannan, was defeated by the next and last of the ancient arrivals, the Milesians from Corunna in north-west Iberia. A shock, so myths have it, that turned the De Dannan into fairies, who then, according to the poets, took occupation of the Newgrange monument.

Occupation has also been claimed for Dagda, the God of all Gods and apparently by Oengus, his cunning son. Despite Dad possessing more power than most, his son was apparently able to trick him out of occupation of his home in the Newgrange mound. No mention was made of what mother's response was to this sudden change in the family habitat.

Unlikely though the myths may be – and in no way suggesting that the underlying stories behind the ancient words are meaningless and do not deserve a place in folklore – a reasonable person would find it difficult to accept that there is no spiritual manifestation within the magic monument.

When you should be so fortunate as to pass along the New-grange passage, to spend some time within the end-chamber, if there is even a tiny nodule of soul beneath your shirt, you will quickly realise that there *is* another plane of existence – with which unusual communication is quite possible. This plane, though, is outside the ambit of this book.

10

The Boyne Valley People

As our attention is solely focused on the great monument on the Newgrange hill, the purpose and usage of *all* other Irish mounds are excluded from these pages. After all, as the ancient monuments were erected over a period of hundreds of years and by a range of people, some of whom may have held differing beliefs and had dissimilar needs, surely it is unreasonable to assume that the hundreds of ancient Irish monuments served the same purpose.

With the above in mind, how is it accepted that the simplest top and sides dolmen and the most complex sun fixed monument can be so  casually lumped together by academia under a general, one-size-fits-all nomenclature, 'tomb?' This classification short-circuits the far more interesting questions, 'What were the Boyne Valley People like and why should they have felt compelled to build such a huge monument at Newgrange? And one with the ground-breaking Sun Window?'

For openers, allow your imagination to travel 5,200 years back in time to Ireland, to the ridge above the Boyne; but to the ridge immediately before the monument had been proposed, let alone constructed. Although it may come as a shock to those who unquestionably accept Hollywood views, not everyone who lived 6,000 years ago was a hairy, low browed, heavily boned, unhygienic grunt.

Certainly, the Boyne Valley People would have scorned and derided this assumption as pure fantasy. Indeed, it could be argued that the major differences between the Boyne Valley People and our arrogant selves are twofold: our wondrous pollution, in politics, religion and the hills of refuse, plus the sophisticated techniques we have developed over the last century to remove our allegedly advanced civilisation from this long-suffering planet.

As a basic premise, it is suggested therefore, that as the Boyne Valley People did successfully build the sun-managing monument, they must have previously developed a deep resource of the Four 'I's' – Imagination, Intelligence, Initiative and Innovation. Attributes that, when the time was ripe and right, perfectly positioned the people of the Boyne to plan, lead, organise and control the design and construction of the mighty edifice. This deed, by itself, should qualify the Boyne Valley People to claim a seat of honour amongst the most advanced civilisations of the time – an accolade so far denied. Nevertheless, at the very least it should be accepted that the Boyne Valley People must have been highly organised and disciplined to have left a monument that was still operative two hundred generations later – a feat that most of today's cement and steel structures may not achieve.

As we examine the evidence of the achievements reached by the ancient Irish more closely, it becomes easier to suspect there may have been other accomplishments that have been overlooked or lost. These attainments could well have been necessary inventions for the successful construction of the monument that now occupies the Newgrange ridge.

Although there is no proof to show that the ancients in Ireland had developed or adopted a means of physically recording information, common sense suggests that some sort of a user-friendly, easy to manage, technique to record data could, and would, have been developed by these innovative and intelligent people. The complexities of balancing the clan's everyday needs with the collection and allocation of the materials required for constructing the monument would have demanded some sort of rudimentary management record.

Examination of the existing 'Boyne Rock Art' shows that a degree of preliminary scratching of the rocks' surfaces preceded the actual chipping and carving of the existing symbols. I suggest, therefore, that it is possible that the step between scratching signs and symbols with a rock onto a rock, and scratching symbols onto a surface with a piece of charcoal or chalk, would not have been too much of a stride for the innovative people of the Boyne. After all, the French Cave Art had appeared on rocky walls before the last Ice Age, thousands of years before the Boyne Valley welcomed the first settlers. Therefore, the possibility of developing an alternative means of making records, while not replacing, but in parallel, to chipping symbols on stones, is a reasonable supposition.

As the Boyne Valley People were already sufficiently advanced to scratch and carve artistic symbols onto the surfaces of rocks, to make 'writing' marks onto a weave of nettles or

Symbols carved into K52, a Newgrange kerbstone

papyrus-type river reed, growing beside the banks of the Boyne, would hardly be taxing. For people who could 'read' the sun and the stars, and were on the verge of building a massive monument with a state-of-the-art attachment, the Sun Window, the art of recording numbers would be easy.

A caveat that nothing has yet been discovered from 5,000 years ago to show that the Boyne Valley People did utilise charcoal or chalk on a perishable writing surface, does not necessarily disprove the possibility. While common sense can recognise possibilities of a form of ogham recordings, time and the climate must also be recognised as powerful erasers. As for the spirals, lozenges, zigzags that do adorn selected stones at Newgrange, these symbols could well represent permanent messages that warranted the effort to record them on stone.

Five and a half thousand years ago, a Time Line comparison of developments between the east and the west of continental Europe would reveal an interesting contrast in philosophy and lifestyles. While the city states between the Tigris and the Euphrates were building their walls, but at the same time collecting great armies to smash them down, it appears the Boyne Valley People were creating a vastly different version of how best to live in harmony not only with each other and their neighbours, but also in learning to cope with the implacable forces of nature.

Dare I suggest the Boyne Valley version may have been somewhat gentler than the heroic violences practised by greedy potentates of Middle East kingdoms that, because of or despite, would produce three of the world's leading, but demonstrably, most aggressive, religions. Although the people of Ireland were somewhat removed from the hot-bed of Middle East activities, it is still likely that there would have been some form of contact. After all, as the clans trekked and sailed along the shores of the Mediterranean Sea, they would surely have retained contact with those who stayed behind.

The likelihood of the retention of these contacts can to some extent be confirmed by the now generally accepted understanding that many European languages can be traced to a common source, spoken around 2000BCE. In other words, communication between the disparate trading tribes of this ancient world could have been far simpler in the third millennium BCE than it is today when the world has given space to the tongues of Babel. Instead of developing their civilisation in isolation, it is likely the Boyne Valley People could have shared the common cup of knowledge being brewed at either end of the Great Middle Sea. It is also likely that there might have been many more established trading links between the early civilisations than presently recognised. These links would have provided opportunities to exchange information on new ideas, innovations and progress; discoveries and insights into astrology, religion, engineering, boat design and construction. Even writing and music could have been amongst the developments exchanged between the Middle East, the Asian sub-continent and the most western continental island.

Unfortunately, many writers of history and archaeology have taken the view that the tide of European civilisation moved only in a westerly direction, ever assuming that whatever was achieved and built in ancient Ireland, was merely a flood residue emanating exclusively from a creative outpouring from one of the academically fashionable Middle East or Mediterranean civilisations. This assumption may not necessarily be accurate.

Indeed, the massive evidence on the Newgrange ridge shows that over 5,000 years ago the ancient Irish had already started the boulders rolling in an achievement that is comparable in many ways with the best that was being constructed at that time throughout the Middle World.

By 3200BCE, a thousand years before Stone Henge was constructed, the Boyne Valley People had started their great venture.

Stone Henge

Apart from the pre-requisite of developing the 4 I's, imagination, intelligence, initiative and innovation, in order to plan and construct the great monument, the Boyne Valley People would need to have reached an advanced social profile. The fact that they were able to build, for its time, the world's most sophisticated Sunscope, shows their society reflected such a desired profile.

*The Boyne Valley People were a highly organised people, sharing a single spiritual belief and well-developed communication skills.
*As they occupied the hills and vales of the Newgrange area for a few thousand years, they were a well-settled people, with deep and stable agrarian roots from which a food surplus would have been the norm.

From these likelihoods, two further meaningful realisations would follow:

*The importance to the Boyne Valley People of the family unit. A well-developed family unit would provide many hands to plant, to harvest, fish, hunt and build, and extra arms to defend the family. The importance of health and fertility would have been well recognised, as would protection and development of their most valuable asset, their children.
*An understanding of the workings and significance of the food chain and their position on this age-old path of nature.

Not only would these insights have triggered the understanding of the importance of reproduction and protection within their own families, they would have extended these concepts to the herds, flocks, crops and undomesticated creatures that fed them.

At the same time, the Boyne Valley People would have worked out the impact the sun exerted upon the fertilisation, growth and survival of all living things. Within the family and without, in the fields and forests, the rivers and the sea 'No sun, no food, no life' would have been almost instinctive knowledge. But, apart from a stable and efficiently organised domestic infrastructure, their external politics would also have had to be successfully organised and maintained. This conclusion can be arrived at from more than one direction. Firstly, the Newgrange monument shows no signs of any form of defence – neither moat nor even decent defensive wall, ditch or ramp, appears to have been built to deter would-be attackers.

Newgrange looking onto the Boyne River

Even the siting of the monument did not incorporate any natural defences – no cliff, no rocky or broken ground, or deep-cut ravine. In fact, to increase the impact of the sun upon the dazzling south-facing white Sun Stones fascia, and the entry of the rays of the winter sun to the end-chamber via the Sun Window, the trees and bushes, even the turf, had been cleared from the acres surrounding the mound. Less than a mile from the Newgrange ridge, the navigation friendly and low-banked Boyne River still curls around the same flat and fertile flood plain. Neither the river nor slope offer any form of protection.

From the north, east and west of the Newgrange ridge, the land is relatively flat and clear of natural obstacles. It could be said, in terms of friendly accessibility, then and now, the New-grange monument offers an air of welcome. In addition, the assumption that the Boyne Valley People lived by an ethos of peace can be concluded from the probable size of the population. Although the rich and fertile country almost certainly afforded a comfortable lifestyle, with sufficient surplus food and fodder for winter storage, there is no sign of a populous settlement. A relatively large resident population around the Newgrange hill of say, 100,000, or more, would have left some sort of indelible domestic marks on the landscape. Other than the monument, the Standing Stones and other ceremonial sites, nothing has been discovered that suggests a large resident population.

Therefore, with but modest numbers available and a large monument to build, the lifestyle of the Boyne Valley People could only have chosen two of the three following options:

Food for the people;

Construction of a complex monument;

Attempted destruction of the neighbours.

In other words, they could have chosen to produce sufficient food to allow permanent occupation of the valleys and hills, including a surplus to be stored for winter

… and to build the mighty monument to honour a deity

… or to raid and fight the neighbours to obtain more of what the Boyne Valley People already possessed.

At that time, gold, silver and rare stones were still well hidden within rock and river.

Should the Boyne clans have opted for raids and wars, the shallow well of their most valuable asset, healthy people and especially the clan's children, would have been rapidly and irrevocably depleted. Domesticated animals, crops and stored supplies, homes; all could be lost to inter-clan fighting. Even victory would not bring lasting rewards, for victory would certainly guarantee future tit-for-tat raids and turn the heady wine of hubris into a poison marked nemesis.

Because there is no sign of the existence of a large population, I contend that the Boyne Valley People would have found it difficult, if not impossible, to:

* farm and find sufficient food,

* fossick and fetch building material for a 200,000 ton mound,

* *and* to initiate and sustain raids and wars *and*, maintain

an effective defence force on permanent standby, while the rest of the able population were away, fetching material for the monument.

Recent geological research has shown that the tons of quartz for the fascia were quarried in the distant Wicklow Mountains and then brought some 80 route miles from the south.* In addition, the young, strong and able would visit the northern shores of Dundalk Bay for the rounded melon size boulders that dot the fascia, another major find and fetch exercise, about 25 route miles to the north. Both journeys were dangerous, onerous and labour intensive exercises that would have required a larger proportion of the younger and stronger clans' people than available had there been a need to retain a permanent home guard in case of raids by neighbours.

However, as the mound *was* built, including mining and fetching the rocks and stones from Wicklow and Dundalk Bay, and as food was obviously supplied to the workers, it would be reasonable to conclude that the Boyne Valley People, and their neighbours, chose to pursue a policy of peace. It is, of course, quite likely that from time to time outsiders may have attempted to attack the Boyne clans. But it is equally likely that a common defence policy on the lines of 'an attack on one was an attack on all' would have been well within their diplomatic arrangements. It is probable that warning fires were laid, primed and manned at strategic points on the hills on both sides of the Boyne River, including the historic Hills of Slane and Tara, to announce an imminent attack.

*Newgrange and the Bend of the Boyne, *Geraldine Stout, pp. 30– 31, Cork University Press 2002.*

I contend that the use of slaves would not have been with-in the culture of peaceful co-existence with the neighbours. After all, slaves rarely volunteer, selfishly demanding to be captured forcibly, usually following a war or undiplomatic raid! In addition, slave labour needs to be housed, fed, guarded, instructed and supervised. These activities would lead to a wasteful squandering of workers and a strain on the resources of the Boyne population. It is quite possible that prisoners taken from foreign raiders would be treated as would livestock. Suitable prisoners would be considered useful additions to the clan's blood stock, and absorbed accordingly.

Therefore, it is more than likely that the Boyne Valley People chose a strategy of peace – leaving themselves time to develop and create a huge and lasting monument.

Montage of symbols

11

Life Expectancy

There is a frequent claim by researchers regarding the availability of labour that life expectancy of the Boyne Valley People would have been in the middle thirties for men, and because of childbirth, slightly earlier for women. Those claims have been based on samples that could be questionable in terms of numbers and whether the samples examined actually represent those responsible for building the monument. In fact, no proof has so far been offered that confirms that the relatively few bones found near Newgrange in any way represent an accurate cross-section of the Boyne Valley People.

Imagine that a researcher, 5,000 years from now, basing a survey into the health and longevity of the twenty-first century Irish people, unwittingly made use of sample bones from a famine graveyard. Although the bones would have been ostensibly from the correct period, the difference between 6850CE and 7000CE being proportionately insignificant, the results would be seriously skewed.

The claims, therefore, that the builders of the mound had short lives because they were unhealthy, or prone to much physical danger, and dead by thirty-five, is hardly underscored by what they planned and built. Sickly people with little expectancy of longevity, would hardly be fired to create great plans for their future. A short lifespan would not be conducive to the positive attitude and persistence demanded to build what the Boyne Valley People did build. Sickly people do not possess the strength to move huge stones or to construct mighty monuments. Great strength and commitment were certainly required to move the 200,000 tons of material, some of it over long distances.

In contrast to the doleful conclusions regarding the well-being and longevity of the Boyne Valley People, I contend that:

* the warmer Irish climate of that time,
* fertile, well-watered lands,
* plenteous food,
* relative geographical isolation from disease and attack from casual raiders,
* wise political unions,
* likely a well-developed knowledge of herbal medicine,
* and lack of stress and chemically stimulated recreations,

would almost certainly have allowed the Boyne Valley People an excellent chance to reach an age of three score years and ten. Maybe even a better chance than, say, the people of the Old Testament tribes recorded at a similar time in history – tribes then wandering the lands of the Tigris and the Euphrates and living in a harsher climate than the ancient Irish but expected to reach three score and ten with ease.

12

The Four Seasons

While the significance of the Winter Solstice was dramatically confirmed by the building of the massive sun sensitive mound, it can be reasonably assumed that all four prime events in the solar year would also have been noted and suitably celebrated with the monument and the Standing Stones as the centrepiece. The Spring Equinox on 21 March, the Summer Solstice on 21 June, the Autumn Equinox on 21 September and the Winter Solstice on 21 December, each date respectively heralding a season, the Season of New Life, the Season of Growth, the Season of Harvest, each annual cycle ending with the Season of Hope, as the people looked forward to the next spring.

Although the two weeks during the Winter Solstice is theoretically in the middle of the northern winter, it is often a period of relative calm before the tempests of January and February set in. This fortnight is known as the halcyon days, so named by sailors and fisher-folk after the legendary seabirds that, during this calmer time, reportedly hatched their eggs whilst floating in great nests upon the deep waters, far from the sight of land. Each year, though, as the days shortened and the autumn days cooled to winter nights, the northern people, then far more than now, would notice the faltering and failing in the food chain: the lack of fruit and berries as trees, bushes and bramble lost the green leaves of summer; the milling emigration of warm weather birds; the disappearance of the rivers' fish to dark and peaceful crevices; the retreat of the wild animals from field and forest, to burrow and lair, to snooze and snore winter's chill away. Even the dark rich soil temporarily lost fertility and strength from the prodding of winter's harsh fingers.

As the northern sun weakened and sank to the lowest aspect in the southern sky, to the Boyne Valley People, in the last months of each annual cycle, it would appear their world was dying. Unless they had made sensible and suitable plans, their future would die with it. It is likely too that, despite the great strides in the development of their imagination, intelligence, initiative and innovation, at year end the Boyne Valley People would feel very exposed to their one great and abiding fear. The fear that as the weakening and cooling sun sank ever lower and lower on the winter horizon, one night it might disappear forever. This possibility would have made both the farmer and fisher very aware of what could happen to the food chain, and the clans' survival, should the sun not re-appear above the far horizon for any length of time.

Although this fear may seem far-fetched in today's knowledge-packed and ever shrinking world, to the people of 5,000 and 7,000 years ago, the possibility was probably more real than any would want to admit. To the Boyne Valley People, if not all the tribes of that time, any climatic or terrestrial event that suggested the return of their sun might be under threat, would quickly sharpen their minds and hone their thoughts to remedial action.

It is possible that a cataclysmic event, involving the apparent disappearance of the sun, might well have taken place just over 5,200 years ago. This occurrence gave the Boyne Valley People such a fright that they were galvanised into a solution that still amazes, and perplexes, virtually ever visitor crossing the Boyne to examine their brilliant response.

While it is, of course, conceded that a major celestial event does provide a somewhat dramatic background against which to stroke the monument to life, it is also possible that something as silent and shirky as the creeping cholera, or yellowing jaundice, may have arrived with an unscreened trader, to do the deathly damage. In fact, some legends contain stories of terrible plagues decimating early settlements in Kerry, Cork and Dublin.

However, as the response of the Boyne Valley People was aimed at their Great God, the Sun, I suggest that whatever stimulated the peaceful people of the Boyne to build the monument, the trigger was likely to be an event from nature, whether climatic, celestial or both and accompanied by the volcanic for good measure.

13

The Trigger

If there is one consistency in nature, it is nature's inconsistency – ask the weathermen, check with the vulcanologist, disturb the furrow-browed fellow fiddling with confusing fission, the response from all three would likely be the same. Just when the safe predictions and proven formulae have been confidentially fed into the great predicting machine, something unexpected will happen. Five thousand years ago, in diametrically opposite parts of the world, a pair of events were separately recorded. Although neither scribe had knowledge of the existence of the other, both reported similar natural disasters.

The Great Flood of the Old Testament – now dated to c3100BCE* – when Noah, his family plus various animals, were able to scramble aboard the huge raft of trees, branches and reeds and safely float above the flooded land between the Tigris and the Euphrates, approximately 50 degrees east (close to where the remnants of the Ma'dan Arabs survive in what is left of the ancient al-Hammar marsh in southern Iraq).

Sir Leonard Woolley's famous flood pit, dug in the same area, revealed a wide band of alluvial silt that corresponds with the circa 3100BCE flood estimate. From the other side of the world, recent deciphering of Mayan records reports a massive

*These dates have been extracted from Legend – The Genesis of Civilisation by David Rohl, Century 1998.

flood to have taken place in Central America, 80 degrees to the west, circa 3100BCE. Add one more date, 3200BCE, the estimated building of the Newgrange monument, almost 10 degrees west, and the time sequence of 3100BCE, 3100BCE and 3200BCE is complete.

The occurrence of the three events could have coincided, Mesopotamia, 50 degrees east and Central America, 80 degrees west, are not too far off equidistant on either side of the Boyne Valley Ireland, 10 degrees west longitude. Surely, it is too much of a co-incidence that both major floods, from either side of the Irish longitude, should be reported to have taken place at virtually the same time, 5,000 years ago. As communications between the two spots, circa 3100BCE, would have been non-existent, cross-pollination of information, with consequent contamination, would have been impossible.

While not suggesting that the two reports refer to the same flood, the root cause of both floods could have been the same event. Whether a huge tectonic shake, or asteroid hit, the inevitable fall-out from either, or both, could have jolted and jarred the Boyne Valley People half to death. It would be possible that a thick cloud of sulphurous smelling debris could have risen, Santorini-like,* thousands of feet into the ancient sky, blotting out the Irish sun and sky as evil clouds circled the globe, convincing the Boyne Valley People that their deepest fear, a disappearing winter sun, was manifesting.

This fear spurred the Boyne Valley People to produce a most creative solution to the feared sun failure. A solution for

* Santorini: Mediterranean town destroyed by a cataclysmic event in ancient times.

which, by developing the Four I's, they had been unconsciously preparing for a project of such magnitude that it would impress and placate the mightiest force in all their world. A concept so big, so startling that it would cool and calm the only force in their understanding powerful enough to save the clans and their future – their Great God, the *Sun*.

The winter sun

14

The Plan

However, despite the impact of whatever it was that shook the Boyne Valley People, it appears they did not believe that simply erecting a huge pile of stones and soil would be sufficient to appease their Great God, the Sun. Although the view from the south bank of the Boyne might suggest that a pile of hastily gathered material was all that was raised, examination of the interior of the Newgrange mound reveals that the leaders of the time created something far more interesting.

The plan they presented to the clans would have had to offer more than simply placating an apparently angry, or unruly god. The plan also needed to dissuade the clans from abandoning their fertile homelands and pleasant lifestyle, and fleeing the seemingly damned place. This act would have loosened forever the strings and strands of the civilisation that had been built up over the many hundreds of years. Therefore, an imaginative and innovative solution would be the minimum that the obviously intelligent Boyne Valley People would accept and be prepared to work at. Anything as inane as to suggest that a heap of hasty rubble would satisfy their Sun God, as well as the clans who would be building her, would almost certainly have found disdainful rejection. Although frightened, the Boyne Valley People were seemingly too advanced, even in a crisis, to accept second best in return for their labours.

The bold evidence on the Newgrange hill proves that the clan leaders came up with what was needed. Examination of the monument at Newgrange shows that what they presented to the clans, and possibly while still affected by the fall-out of the catastrophic event, elicited a response so powerful that it led to one of the greatest creative leaps the human race had thus far attempted.

Whatever the causal event of the crisis, violent earthquake, a storm of unimaginable intensity, a collision from suicidal asteroid, even a sneaky disease, it is likely that the aftermath did not quickly disappear, thereby allowing forgetfulness and complacency to dilute the content of nature's fearsome message. It is possible that the awful event lingered on, turning days into nights: fine particles of dust colouring the rain a bloody red; balls of hail and falls of fish and frogs, pelting from a jet black sky. The horrors could have been many, and all interfering with the established patterns of the growing, harvesting and hunting seasons. Whether or not the shocking occurrence was related to the two ancient floods, or if Co. Meath received a more personal celestial visitor, is not too important. A massive monument does not arise from a somnambulant people. Something dramatic must have so stimulated the Boyne Valley People that they invoked the fullest stretch of their talents and the Four I's to create what they did, over 5,000 years ago.

Their plan, in broad terms, was to arrange a union between the two most powerful entities in the world, to be celebrated each year within a soon-to-be-built and massive monument.

15

You, the Leader

Before the union could be formally arranged, there would first have to be the little matter of designing and building the venue for the ceremony and the place for the consummation, the nuptial nest.

In order to make the 200,000 ton challenge more personal, you are invited to assume the mantle of leader of the clan-in-residence on the Newgrange hill, 5,200 years ago. Your brief from the College of Elders would be to present the operational plan to erect the monument, including logistical details, so that everyone would know what had to be done, by whom, where, when and how. At the same time, your clan, and participating clans, would need to continue with whatever activities were required to keep the people healthy and happy.

As you faced the many hundred pairs of eyes, you would have to steer a careful path, one wrong step and everything would be off, and maybe your head as well! Although the urgent need to placate nature's unrestrained elements will help, your clans' people will not be a push-over for an idea that could threaten their established living patterns, or leave their children exposed to danger. They may rather emigrate than face the unruly forces presently disturbing their peace.

However, as the clan did build the monument, you must have spoken well to the resourceful and practical people, not easily swayed by foolish promises of wispy visions that may dissolve under scrutiny.

The monument now standing proudly on the hill shows that your reasoning and method of building was accepted; not only by your own clan, but also by the neighbouring clans who would, inevitably, become involved in one way or another – either by taking part in the building and the ensuing ceremonies, or by continuing to support the long established ethos of peace so that building would be possible. But most important of all, your presentation needed to make sense a week, a month, even some years later, after the initial excitement and wonder of the concept had cooled and hardened. The motivation would need to survive the long, damp, cold dawn, when the sizzle of the initial excitement could have cooled to slush.

As newly proclaimed leader you would have successfully persuaded your fellow clans' people to allocate large slices of their time and energy to find and to fetch a host of rocks and half a million stones, including boulders weighing up to ten tons. All had to be dragged from hills and valleys from miles around and to a seemingly random spot on a ridge. Hundreds of water-rounded melon-shaped stones had to be found by scouring riverbeds and rocky seashores.

Tons of quartz Sun Stones had to be mined, by antler and by hand, in the Wicklow Mountains, some 80-route miles south of the Bend in the Boyne. The return journey, first down the mountain's slopes, avoiding lakes and rivers, then across the hilly coastal plain, to a loading spot on a part of the east coast that is not known for safe coves. Once the chunks of quartz had been carefully loaded onto the relatively frail craft, they had to be shipped north, by current, by oar and by sail, first up the coast in boats fashioned from wooden frames, reeds and tightly stretched cowhides, past Dublin-to-be and on to the mouth of the Boyne, near where busy Drogheda stands today. The penultimate task would be to move the quartz and melon-shaped boulders up the Boyne, against the swiftly running river, to the final stage – ox-pulled sledges across the flood plain to the ridge and designated deposit area, close to the precise spot where astronomers had calculated the Newgrange edifice containing the end-chamber, should be built.

But while the far-flung fields were being raided for building materials, closer to home things would also have been buzzing. All the usual aspects of clan life, farming, hunting, fishing, weaving, sewing and educating, would have been continuing undisturbed – the usual clan requirements with seasonal variations. The plan you would have presented would add an omnibus of extra duties to their daily schedules: locating and fetching the two metre stone slabs to provide the uprights, the orthostats, to line the inner walls of the passage and end-chamber; finding, carrying and dragging the large flagstones for the ceiling of the passage and to corbel the end-chamber. Collecting and delivering thousands of smaller stones and soil, for the 200,000 ton mound that would later cover the passage and end-chamber.

As leader, you would have delegated various responsibilities: organising the sledges, the production of hundreds of skin bags to carry the soil and smaller stones and persuading nimble fingers to find and twist nettle and hair into knots for the many metres of ropes that would be required. There would be the few hectares of turves to be cleared from the building site, squares of grass to be later used by the builders of the mound as a stabilising filling between the layers of supporting and covering stones. While you were planning that, and in between sorting out hiccups along the way, you would quickly realise that you had no calculator, radio communications, spade, steel pick, bulldozer, etc.

The point on the southern horizon, where the December sun halted before turning to rise progressively further east, would need to be clearly marked to assist plotting the inclination and the direction of the dawn rays. The features of the monument could then be correctly aligned, horizontally and vertically, to receive the Winter Solstice sun. In this task, the team could not afford even half an oops! To consider moving the monument once the passage stones had been planted, and the Sun Window constructed would be enough to make those responsible lose more than their minds.

Meantime, stone masons, with only stone tools, would be marking and chipping water gullies into the flat stones destined for the ceiling of the passage in order to keep the interior dry. At the same time, more artistic masons would be creating symbols and patterns on selected stone surfaces.

As leader, you would also have to deal with the inevitable accidents, an errant stone, a sinking boat, a breaking rope, or painful confrontation with an unmannered beast.

Once you had outlined what the clans would be doing in their spare time for at least the next eight plus years, adding a year here and there for bad weather, do you really believe that your colleagues would take you seriously if you then advised that the project was actually to store the corpse, or ash, of someone who might conveniently die just as the mighty monument was completed – whenever that might be! Newgrange was, of course, built hundreds of years before the pharaohs had their mausoleums dug into the Egyptian sands. It is likely, therefore, that the cult of uber-ego never did infect Neolithic Ireland.

The suggestion that the huge mound was to be erected to commemorate the anticipated death of a single person, or even a family, would likely be received as fanciful and treated in a manner best understood by down-to-earth farmers. As for a suggestion that the monument was built after the death of an individual, but the body would be stored until the massive mound had been completed, apart from the rapid deterioration and physical humiliation of what might once have been an elegant and awesome leader, such a proposal would surely have stretched the pragmatic credulity of the Boyne inhabitants. Even if travellers from the dry Middle East had recommended mummification as a means of preserving a body, Ireland's damper climate would almost certainly have proved an insurmountable obstacle. Fortunately for posterity, as the plan that you presented to the clans was based on life and living, a message which farmers could support, five millennia later we are still able to visit and marvel at what you and your teams achieved on the Newgrange ridge.

16

The Farmer's View

Regarding life and death, a decent method of disposing of the dead during the long tenure at Newgrange would have been an established custom of the civilised Boyne Valley People. Then, as now, and throughout the world, it is also likely that the prosperous agrarian community measured their wealth in living numbers. As a peaceful farming people, the Boyne Valley People would instinctively have chosen fresh life over unproductive dull death. A farmer's philosophy, 'the dead don't milk cows' and supplemented by the corollary, 'only the living catch live fish', could have represented the likely attitude of the Boyne Valley People 5,000 and 6,000 years ago.

Therefore, there is good reason to assume that the joy of life, tempered with due respect for those who have passed on, would probably be the dominating creed of the peaceful and creative people of the Boyne. A cult of the dead, as suggested in some quarters, would have been anathema. In addition, when it is remembered that their homes were constructed from poles, branches, latticed mud-fill and thatch roofs, to waste good farming, hunting and fishing time constructing a huge stone house for a dead person, alive or dead at the time, well …

Fortunately, the solution that the leaders worked out to solve whatever major event had challenged the future of the clans, was based on life not death. It was a choice that caused the vibrant agricultural community living beside the Boyne, to build a monument that celebrated life and living in their hope-filled tomorrow, rather than death in dull yesterdays.

17

Building Her

During the 1962–75 excavation and restoration of the New-grange monument, it became apparent that the passage with the Sun Window, and the end-chamber with the cleverly corbelled ceiling, had been constructed as two separate, though joined up, entities. It is also possible that, although ramps would have been formed to assist the placement of the ceiling slabs over the passage, and the corbelling of the end-chamber, pressure to complete the 'operational' aspects of the monument could have delayed the building of the vast enclosing mound.

It is surmised that because the event that triggered the construction of the great mound was particularly frightening, the Boyne Valley People may have been anxious to commence the ceremonies as soon as possible and were unwilling to delay their plan to dissuade the sun from again leaving their world for a length of time that might threaten the clans' survival. Consequently to save time, the Newgrange monument may have been declared open for business as a naked stone construction. At this stage the edifice would comprise the passage, Sun Window and end-chamber, but without the massive drum shaped mound. The construction ramps would have been removed once the cap-stone of the corbelled ceiling had been put in place.

It would have been a somewhat stark temple without the time and labour-consuming quartz-stacked fascia and mound.

Nevertheless, the unclad monument would have offered a most arresting sight above the Boyne and one that, then as now, would attract fascinated visitors from great distances. I surmise that some of the ancient visitors to Newgrange may have constructed their own versions on returning home to lands to the east.

The two-part construction, without the mound, would mean that the delay between the selling of the concept to the clans and the first entry of the dawn beams of the winter sun, through the Sun Window and up the passage to the end-chamber, could have been sooner than expected. Once the plans had been explained to the clans' people and the initial positioning measurements completed, the main limitation to activity on the project would have been the availability of hands, especially during the sowing and harvesting seasons. It is likely that even while the manifestations of the cause of the raising of the monument were still lingering above and around the Boyne Valley, the finding and fetching of monument material would have commenced.

Having measured and marked the relative direction between the position and height of the stone basin and the Sun Window, the building of both parts would proceed simultaneously. The passage and Sun Window could be built together while the end-chamber, together with her three flanking alcoves and the characteristic corbelled ceiling, would be built towards the passage, eventually to be joined into a free-standing monument.

In the context of the building of the end-chamber, the corbelled ceiling has been hailed as both attractive and cleverly executed. While undoubtedly true, considering the area of the end-chamber, a gradually closing (and also, of course, concomitant rising) of the roof would have been about the only safe and long-term means of providing a leak-proof covering of the approximately 30 square metre room.

As suggested earlier, the third stage, the massive mound, was added after the urgent business of placating raging elements had been achieved to the satisfaction of the Boyne Valley People, when they would have had more time to find and fetch the huge quantity of additional material.

During the 1962–75 restoration, a number of decorated surfaces facing away from the passage and end-chamber and directly into the covering mound were exposed to view for the first time in 4,000 years. This apparent anomaly has often raised the obvious question – why would the builders purposely hide stones their colleagues had painstakingly decorated? A fair question that could be answered by the possibility – because of impatience to start the ceremonies as soon as possible – the original, or at least the first version of the Newgrange monument had, indeed, been planned to be free-standing and without the present covering mound. The symbolic messages carved into the stones, to be later obscured by the mound, would at first, have been in full view.

Later when a decision was made to put the covering mound in place, it would have been realised that a major re-construction would be required to re-position the decorated stones that were about to be covered. It might then have been decided that to re-position the decorated stones was not worth the effort. At this time it may also have been decided the messages given by the about-to-be covered symbols were either no long-er relevant and could be covered, or would still be effective, even if covered.

In other words, farmers' practicality might well have won the day. Again!

During the 1962–1975 excavation it was also discovered that a mantle of rounded stones, each about 30 cms in dia-meter and different from the usual cairn fill, had been placed to surround part of the outside of the rising 'ceiling' of the end-chamber – almost like an open scarf. Examination show-ed that these remarkably uniform boulders rested upon a large lintel over the passage but the roof of the passage did not sup-port this lintel. This discovery would support the suggestion* that the passage, Sun Window and end-chamber were, for a time, used as a complete, free-standing monument and that the mound was added, or at least completed, some time after the passage, Sun Window and end-chamber had been in use.

* *see* Newgrange *by Michael O'Kelly p. 99*

18

Fusion

Debating whether or not placating wild and wanton elements of nature was the trigger that galvanised the Boyne Valley People into creating the monument, should not distract from another important consideration. Not only is it likely that whatever started the creative juices of the Boyne Valley People needed to have been huge and compelling to justify what was created on the ridge, there must have also have been a single individual, 5,200 years ago, who sparked the process that resulted in the building of the huge monument.

A strong-minded and highly intelligent individual who, over breakfast one quite ordinary morning, first said to partner and mate, 'We should build the greatest and grandest monument anyone could imagine. And then what has been troubling us, will hopefully trouble us no more.' Thereafter, whomever that individual may have been, first the family, then the neighbours, followed by the neighbours' neighbours, and finally the leader and advisers, all would have to be convinced of the necessity of building a 200,000 ton monument. This was a sales task made even more challenging as the target market, the clans, were not simply agreeing to a 'someone-else-will-do-the-job' proposal. They were agreeing to, and accepting, a personal commitment that would require each to find and collect tons of inedible, unwearable stones, rather than plant, find and collect food, while at the same time completing other demanding day-to-day tasks.

Whoever the unknown individual may have been who sparked the concept, male or female, it is deep within the mound that the Boyne Valley People really brought their brilliant solution to life. Although the plan was simple to comprehend, it would not be easy to execute and would require a fusion of the Four I's – initiative, imagination, intelligence and innovation – to a new level.

It appears to me that the plan the Boyne Valley People finally formulated was so far removed from what is usually expected by latter day investigators, that the academic disciplines employed are not able to detect what Newgrange is all about. Could it be that those who seek and search amongst ancient ruins, while carefully following techniques designed to preserve that being examined, are so caught up by the application of the classic disciplines, that in the case of Newgrange, they are unable to recognise what the Boyne Valley People had really created?

After all, which of the 'ologies' is geared to recognise the signs of an arranged marriage between two out-of-world entities? It is hardly their business. Such an esoteric revelation would probably require the input and insight of a mystic, rather than highly qualified and dedicated Masters of the Arts and the Sciences.

19

The Marriage

Few marriages are casually arranged. A wedding is an event that involves much consideration and often deep, conflicting emotions. It has, of course, been often coined that marriages are made in heaven. It could equally be noted that most weddings are planned in the kitchen.

Clear evidence on the Newgrange ridge plainly suggests that over 5,000 years ago the Boyne Valley People proposed a marriage to overcome whatever it was that was interfering with the local food chain and endangering the clan's very existence. However, this marriage could not be an 'ordinary' pairing between two rich or ruling families. The needs of the time were considered far too onerous for a mere mortal marriage. Having analysed the apparent causes and the manifestation of the tribulations that had been visited upon them, the leader, the keeper and the elders evidently decided to apply a large measure of the Four I's, and look outside the traditional parameters of custom and precedent.

The marriage that the imaginative Boyne Valley People had in mind would be a union between the only parties sufficiently powerful to alleviate whatever it was that threatened the clan's existence. A union that would be honoured and celebrated every year, thereby binding the partners ever closer, and at the same time reminding the clans of their own duties and obligations towards the wedded pair. The Boyne Valley People would contrive a wedding between the Great God, the Sun and the Earth Mother. This union, so they believed, would provide the solution to whatever terrible event had assaulted and damaged their food chain and threatened their future existence in the warm and fertile hills and vales that surround the Boyne.

But where is the evidence? What are the signs that suggest such an ambitious wedding? How did the Boyne Valley People manage to invoke and involve the bride and groom? Was the wedding pure ritual, or did consummation occur? And where and how did this all take place? Good questions all and ones that require answers.

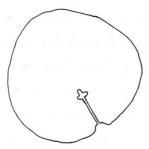

Aerial view of the Newgrange Mound

This is a bird's eye view of the Newgrange monument. The passage, end-chamber and alcoves extending almost a third of the way into the mound. Imagine that the Newgrange mound was created to represent the bride, the Earth Mother. Accordingly, the end-chamber would represent the womb and the alcoves the ovaries – the basins in the alcoves ready to hold the symbolic 'eggs' chosen to be fertilised. During consummation, entry to the womb could only be reached via the Sun Window and along the passage leading to the end-chamber, or more accurately, the nuptial chamber.

The Great God, the Sun, would play the part of the groom and as is the way with terrestrial weddings, although theoretically of equal importance, on the 'great day' the groom would have his dance carefully choreographed so that his role would appear more supportive.

As far as the entrance below the Sun Window is concerned, only the keeper and a few selected assistants, trained to carry out the necessary activities required before and after consummation had been achieved, could enter. In effect, this was little different from the ministrations of a modern gynaecologist. To ensure that the privacy of the end-chamber did not suffer unauthorised invasion, a tightly fitting, heavy stone door deterred would-be molesters. This huge stone door can still be seen, to the right of the entrance to the monument.

Because the cataclysmic event had interfered with their food chain, the symbolic act of marriage was arranged to take place in the dead of winter, when the life fluids within the food chain were at their lowest and the food supply the most vulnerable. It was a union designed to light the fuse of fertility and fire the re-birth of each ensuing New Year and reinstitute the food chain that might have been seriously interrupted by

The Stone Door

whatever calamity or major event had disrupted the lives of the Boyne Valley People.

In modern terms, the wedding celebrations would take place for six days, on either side of the longest night of the year, 21–22 December, the Winter Solstice in the northern hemisphere.

Just as most formal marriages are preceded by sessions of rehearsal, instructions, counselling and various social activities, pre-nuptial Newgrange events also commenced a few days before the northern Winter Solstice period. At the start of the solstice period, the clans could have been regaled by stories of the events that led to the building of the massive monument and peppered with catechisms covering the clan's responsibilities and duties to the bride and groom. During this time the Newgrange hill could also have been the venue to a host of other more entertaining activities, dancing, singing and staged events depicting fertility and reproduction. It should not be overlooked that the Boyne Valley People lived much closer to real nature than the citizens of today's developed world. Accordingly, while some of their dances and fertility enactments might cause the righteous upholders of our modern morals to send outraged missives to the broadsheets, it is also likely that certain of our modern activities would equally astonish and amaze our ancient forebears.

However, the day before the first rays of the dawn sun were due to penetrate to the end-chamber, one of the most important parts of the ceremonies would take place – the careful placing of offerings by the keeper into the three stone basins in the alcoves, deep within the mound. Offerings of seeds, roots, dried fruits, leaves, human and animal forms made from twisting and weaving grass, each and all representing some part of the fertility ladder and food chain.

Regarding the actual consummation, the careful construction of the Sun Window would limit the groom's penetration to the time of sunrise, when the male is the most single-minded and potent. For seventeen minutes each day, the dawn rays of the Great God, the Sun would stretch over the southern hills, to enter the Earth Mother through the private portal and reach deep into the nuptial chamber, providing a soft ethereal light of other world magic to symbolically fertilise the eggs of his bride, the Earth Mother.

This brilliantly conceived solution by the Boyne Valley People explains the reality for building the mighty temple, Newgrange – the Temple to Life.

When you visit Newgrange, you too may realise that you are entering the manifestation of one of the world's most ambitious concepts – the marriage between the all-powerful Sun, without which life in any form would be impossible, and our Earth Mother, herself the generous provider of all the gifts that we can ever require.

Because the concept to placate their Great God, the Sun was built on fertility, birth and growth, it is not surprising there are no signs of burial goods, or the stains of blood sacrifices, upon the stone basins in the end-chamber. There is no passage grave at Newgrange, in contrast there is a massive Temple to Life.

20

Where did they go?

Although it appears that the builders of the Newgrange monument, the Temple to Life, disappeared without leaving a forwarding address, a tantalising clue of what might have happened may be emerging. A clue has been discovered in Egypt of an event that appears to have taken place circa 2100BCE. Researchers claim to have found evidence that about 4,000 years ago, a prolonged and freezing cold weather pattern spilt south from the arctic circle, temporarily altering European weather patterns, even managing to reach and ruin the people living on the middle Nile by turning Egyptian farmland into a dustbowl.

If shockingly cold weather could so interfere with life along the Nile to destroy a well-established kingdom, the effect of a significant period of freezing weather on the ancient Irish, more than 30 degrees latitude further north, would have been devastating. The fertile Boyne Valley and all Ireland would have been turned from a green and warm land of agricultural surpluses, into a sub-arctic wasteland within a few years.

So, faced with a ferocious climatic onslaught, and apparently abandoned by their Great God, the Sun, the Boyne Valley People would have been forced from their once lovely lands, including their magic Temple to Life, to move to warmer climes. Unsurprisingly then, that apart from the huge monument, there are few traces of the homes of the advanced civilisation that built the Temple to Life and dominated the north-eastern corner of ancient Ireland before circa 2200BCE.

As for signs of their homes along the Boyne, snow, ice and polar winds over only a few years, would effectively obliterate almost all evidence of homes built of wattle, mud-filled walls and roofed with grasses and reeds. Even highly localised geophysical surveys, using state-of-the-art magnetometric equipment, would have difficulty revealing traces long hidden under the ploughed swathes of Newgrange farmlands.

It will probably never be known what caused the collapse of part of the mound so that the entrance and Sun Window became blocked. The important point is that the blocking of the two points of entry saved the Temple to Life from depredations by thieves, squatters and souterrain diggers that damaged other monuments in the area.

This is a suitable opportunity to reiterate that the monuments at Knowth and Dowth, and in fact, the hundreds of stone circles, standing stones, caves, cromlechs and dolmens, have been excluded from this proposition for a practical reason. To follow tradition and bundle the whole lot together as tombs can only result in confusion and inaccurate conclusions. In some cases, for example Knowth, over many years, the monument was altered to satisfy different uses. The Temple to Life at Newgrange escaped that fate until as recently as 1699, when the entrance, but not the Sun Window, was discovered

But as to the final destination of these wonderful people, Ireland's first civilisation to leave a lasting mark, who knows?

Having developed the Four I's to the level of successfully constructing a temple that is still in working order after five thousand years, surely they were too astute to meekly perish on a freezing hillside. After all they had achieved, it would be difficult to believe that they softly vanished.

Is it possible that they were able to take their accumulated knowledge of moving and building with large stones, of the movements of the sun, of agrarian practices, even of herbal medicines, and maybe also of politically promoted peace, and sail towards the newest centre of progressive civilisation, the middle Nile and Egypt circa 2100BCE? There to harness a different weather, there to meet the Boat People, as they pushed west from the Red Sea and the turmoil of ancient Mesopotamia, ready to take occupation of Egypt.

In the past, as in the future, with logic and luck, all things are possible.

CHRIS O'CALLAGHAN

IRISH SYMBOLS
OF 3500 BC

N. L. Thomas

The riddle of the inscriptions at Newgrange, Knowth and other equally ancient Irish sites in the Boyne valley have been partly deciphered at last.

The inscribed passage mound stones tell of prehistoric man's concept of the world: the flat earth with a hemispherical bowl overhead, the sun and the moon circling round.

The legends and myths of Ireland can be directly related to the stone engravings; certain numbers such as nine, eleven, seventeen, twenty-seven and thirty-three are common to both. These numbers have important symbolic meanings as well as their numerical values.

The oldest calender in the history of mankind is portrayed – sixteen months of 22 or 23 days, four weeks of five days each month, eight annual solar and seasonal events. It has been known for some time that the passages into the Newgrange and Knowth mounds are aligned with sunrise and sunset on the solstitial and equinoctial days each year. They are the cornerstones of the sixteen month calender and the eight annual festival days.

The evidence from 3500BC to 3200BC precedes British calender building sites at Mount Pleasant 2600BC and Stonehenge 2000BC.

A HANDBOOK OF CELTIC ORNAMENT

John G. Merne

A complete course in the construction and development of Celtic ornament with over 700 illustrations. *A Handbook of Celtic Ornament* takes basic symbols or ideographs and develops them into a systemised method of construction for most forms of Celtic decoration.

Apart from its value as a drawing textbook this book will be of immense value to all students of Arts and Crafts. The Merne method for the construction and development of Celtic ornament has not been surpassed and this book is a challenge both to the student and the professional artist to take part of our tradition and make it their own, to use, to repeat, but most of all to develop.

THE COURSE OF IRISH HISTORY

Edited by T. W. Moody and F. X. Martin

A revised and enlarged version of this classic book provides a rapid short survey, with geographical introduction, of the whole course of Ireland's history. Based on a series of television programmes, it is designed to be both popular and authoritative, concise but comprehensive, selective but balanced and fair-minded, critical but constructive and sympathetic. A distinctive feature is its wealth of illustrations.

An Introduction to
Irish High Crosses

Hilary Richardson & John Scarry

The Irish high crosses are the most original and interesting of all the monuments which stud the Irish landscape. They are of international importance in early medieval art. For their period there is little to equal them in the sculpture of western Europe as a whole.

This beautiful book gives basic information about the crosses. A general survey is followed by an inventory to accompany the large collection of photographs which illustrate their variety and richness. In this way readers will readily have at their disposal an extensive range of the images created in stone by sculptors working in Ireland over a thousand years ago.

Things Irish

Anthony Bluett

Things Irish provides the reader with an entertaining and informative view of Ireland, seen through the practices, beliefs and everyday objects that seem to belong specifically to this country. Discarding the usual format of chapters on a variety of themes, the book uses short descriptive passages on anything from whiskey to standing stones, from May Day to hurling, in order to create a distinctive image of Irish life. The reader is free to roam from topic to topic, from passage to passage, discovering a wealth of new and surprising facts and having a number of misguided beliefs put right.

THE SHEELA-NA-GIGS OF IRELAND AND BRITAIN
The Divine Hag of the Christian Celts

Joanne McMahon & Jack Roberts

Sheela-na-gigs are carvings of female images depicted as naked and posing in a provocative manner which accentuate the most powerfully evocative symbol of the vulva. They were erected on many churches of the medieval period and were almost invariably placed in a very prominent position such as over the main entrance door or a window.

This book is written from a non-academic perspective and the illustrated catalogue section is a very comprehensive alphabetically listed reference to all known sheela-na-gigs in Ireland and Britain.

THE GREAT IRISH FAMINE

Edited by Cathal Póirtéir

This is the most wide-ranging series of essays ever published on the Great Irish Famine and will prove of lasting interest to the general reader. Leading historians, economists, geographers – from Ireland, Britain and the United States – have assembled the most up-to-date research from a wide spectrum of disciplines, including medicine, folklore and literature, to give the fullest account yet of the background and consequences of the Famine.